Golden Words

PROVERBS AND SAYINGS THAT EVERYONE NEEDS

Golden Words for Man and Woman
Golden Letters
Gold Worth of Words

ALI SUROOR

authorHOUSE®

AuthorHouse™
1663 Liberty Drive
Bloomington, IN 47403
www.authorhouse.com
Phone: 833-262-8899

Published by AuthorHouse 09/30/2021

ISBN: 978-1-6655-3870-1 (sc)
ISBN: 978-1-6655-3880-0 (e)

Print information available on the last page.

Any people depicted in stock imagery provided by Getty Images are models,
and such images are being used for illustrative purposes only.
Certain stock imagery © Getty Images.

This book is printed on acid-free paper.

Because of the dynamic nature of the Internet, any web addresses or links contained in
this book may have changed since publication and may no longer be valid. The views
expressed in this work are solely those of the author and do not necessarily reflect the
views of the publisher, and the publisher hereby disclaims any responsibility for them.

Introduction

Dear Readers,

Yes, this book will surely enrich your
frame of reference and may satisfy
your intellectual reservoirs.
I have the pleasure to put forward some
literature extracts combining examples,
proverbs, guidance wisdom which I hope,
may reach your beautiful hearts.
I am using it as a ladder to reach
your high intellectual esteem.

Is there any space in our intellectual
memory to help us to move within?
Is it possible that tomorrow witnesses
the activation of our stagnant affairs?
Are there answers to our recurring
questions to satisfy our curiosity
with convincing answers?
Yes, or No?
Are we all hiding the answers?
These are for sure, solid facts!

Dedication

To everyone who has touched
this book, I say:

I am proud to be present through
this book in your generous hands
When we release meditation with calm
freedom, all the values of spiritual
serenity are represented before us
The colors overlap in a rare
philosophical way
It paints us the true meanings
of the pure world
Everyone has a different ability to
read the creative landscape
This is what makes people like
rainbows different with love,
purity and cooperation.

SOULS ARE LIKE FLOWERS, SOME OF THEM
EMIT PERFUMES, AND SOME OF THEM ARE
SATISFIED WITH FORM WITHOUT SCENT,
WE MUST NOT UPROOT EITHER FLOWER
RATHER, WE HAVE TO STAND AT THE
REASONS WHY THE TWO FLOWERS DO
NOT GROW AND TREAT THEM
NOT ALL PEOPLE ARE ALIKE
THERE IS SO MUCH IN THE HUMAN SPIRIT THAT
WE HAVE NOT YET BEEN ABLE TO DECIPHER
BUT WHAT DO WE HAVE AS HUMAN BEINGS?
IT IS JUST LOVE.

Golden Words for Man and Woman

REVELATIONS OF MY PEN!!!

WILL THE HUMBLE LOVE WIN,

OR THE VICTORY WILL <u>PREVAIL</u>

WITH ARROGANT RICHNESS?

MIND ALWAYS LOOKS BEYOND

THE EYE GLASSES.

DO THE GOOD AND PROCEED, WAIT

NO GRATITUDE FROM ANY ONE.

Aiming sharply towards women's hearts requires money, <u>A FANCY</u> car and a speechless tongue.

LOVE IS GONE, MONEY IS GONE, THE MONEY IS BACK, BUT LOVE ISN'T.

When you <u>have</u> an empty glass in your hand, and the river is far away, don't expect <u>anybody</u> to fill it for you, you must go and fill it yourself. No money will knock on your door if you don't work.

I HAVE THE KEY FOR ALL KIND
AND SIMPLE HEARTS.

BRAIN HUNGER IS MORE PAINFUL
THAN THE HUNGER OF STOMACH.

ENDEAVORING TRUE LOVE IS
SIMILAR TO TRYING TO PASS A
THREAD THROUGH THE NEEDLE
IN A STORMY WEATHER.

MONEY MAY BRING LOVE, BUT LOVE
IS NOT ALWAYS BROUGHT BY MONEY.

HAPPINESS IS A BRILLIANT
MOTTO ADOPTED BY OPTIMISTIC
PEOPLE INCLUDING ME.

THE PEN DOESN'T WRITE BY
ITSELF, SO IS THE EXCELLENCE,
NEVER GAINED WITH NO PAIN.

POSH CARS ARE THE MOST
FAVORABLE FOR WOMEN, I DO HAVE A
POSH CAR, BUT IT IS IN THE GARAGE.

BEAUTY IN LIFE LIES IN
MINUTE DETAILS.

You can compensate everything,
but <u>you</u> can't retrieve a minute
you missed in your life.

I AM TIED WITH LOVE, YET
I AM A FREE BIRD.

I SHALL NOT MARRY UNTIL THE
SUN APPEARS IN THE MIDDLE
OF THE NIGHT, PLEASE DON'T
ASK ME WHY. FULL STOP.

When the wind is wild, sails should not resist, so when your boss is furious, keep quiet until it's quiet again.

A BULLET DOESN'T SELECT ITS TARGET. IT'S THE MAN BEHIND IT WHO DEFINES ITS COURSE, SO, YOU HAVE TO CHOOSE WHAT DO YOU WANT IN THIS WORLD, YET, DON'T REFUSE THE HONEST ADVICE AS WELL.

UNIVERSITY EQUALS EDUCATION
AND LIFE IS A UNIVERSITY. THE
MORE YOU LEARN IN UNIVERSITIES,
THE MORE YOUR INTELLECTUAL
LIFE PROLONGS AND THE MORE YOU
LIVE, THE MORE YOU LEARN. THEY
BOTH LEAD TO THE SAME RESULT.

HELLO WOMAN, IF YOU ARE SEEKING A HUSBAND I'LL GIVE YOU AN ADVICE: DON'T MAKE YOUR HEART A DONATION BOX SINCE THE RETURN OF THE BOX WILL BE GONE TO A GROUP OF POOR PEOPLE. MAKE YOUR HEART LIKE A LOTTERY BOX, SO THE WINNER WILL BE JUST ONE. DON'T TRUST MEN'S ROMANTIC WORDS.

THE <u>GIRL</u> WHO <u>LOOK</u> AT YOUR SHOES IS OFTEN A MATERIAL GIRL. THE GIRL WHO DOESN'T ASK HOW MUCH YOU EARN MONTHLY IS MORE INTERESTED IN YOUR MIND

ALL HUMANS ARE EQUAL, BUT THEIR MINDS ARE DIFFERENT

I F A PIECE OF WOOD COULD TALK, IT WOULD TELL US HOW PAINFUL THE NAILS, BUT DESTINY MADE IT MUTE.

DON'T MAKE YOUR IMPRESSION IN THE HEARTS OF PEOPLE LIKE FOOT PRINTS, <u>AS</u> WIND WILL REMOVE <u>THEM</u>, MAKE IT LIKE A TATTOO ON THE SKIN, HARD TO REMOVE.

THE FISH HOOK DOESN'T DEFINE
WHAT FISH TO HOOK, AND SO IS
WOMEN CHOICES OF MEN, SOMETIME
HOOKS UNFAVORABLE FISH.

PHILOSOPHY IS A POSTURE OF
MENTAL SUPERIORITY AND NOT
NECESSARILY A KIND OF MADNESS
AS CLAIMED BY THOSE WHO ARE
NOT AWARE THAT INDUSTRY IS
THE OFFSPRING OF INNOVATIVE
PHILOSOPHY SCIENCES.

SMILE WHILE IT'S FREE, BECAUSE SMILE WILL OPEN THE ROAD TO <u>PROJECTS</u> THAT MAY BRING YOU REAL PROFITS IN THE FUTURE.

SINCERE EMOTIONS RE JUST LIKE A JASMIN FLOWER THAT GIVES IT SCENTS TO EVERY PASSING BREATHE FOR FREE.

When ideas mingle, facts are lost and the mind gets confused and distracted. The only way to keep up is to isolate from everything until the devil is gone and angles start to appear.

IF YOU DON'T WANT TO SEE BAD
PEOPLE, WEAR THE IGNORING
GLASSES WHEN MEETING ANY OF
THOSE DEPRESSING PEOPLE.

Don't say harsh words lest
you may hurt someone. Not all
hearts can tolerate pain. Be
quiet <u>to avoid</u> losing everything.

Melody is a play that interprets the <u>feelings</u> of those who don't know <u>how</u> to express their feelings in writing. The rose doesn't speak, but its scent is more expressive

MONEY MAY BRING HAPPINESS
WHICH COULD BE TEMPORARY
BECAUSE THOSE WHO GATHER
AROUND THE WEALTHY PERSON
WILL HAVE THEIR OWN GREED
AND NOT TRUE FRIENDS.

MARRIAGE IS THE SACRED BOND
BETWEEN MAN AND WOMAN,
WHAT RESTRAINS PARENTS IS
THE PRESENCE OF CHILDREN,
AS THEIR MOTTO WILL BE THE
IDEAL RESPONSIBILITY.

FINDING A FAITHFUL FRIEND
NOWADAYS IS MORE VALUABLE
THAN FINDING A TREASURE.

WRITE, WRITE AND WRITE. DON'T
BE JUST BE A READER. LEARN
HOW TO DO THINGS, TO PRODUCE.
DON'T ADAPT YOURSELF TO THE
CULTURE OF CONSUMERS.

You don't have to always succeed, sometimes, failure is the first step <u>towards</u> success. So learn how to be patient and not rush things.

THE DEFINITION OF ALCOHOL:
THEY ARE ELEMENTS COMPOSED
OF OBLIVION, ILLUSIONS, AND
TEMPORARY HAPPINESS FOR THE
PURPOSE OF ESCAPING A FINANCIAL
OR EMOTIONAL PROBLEM.

WHEN YOU SEARCH INSIDE YOURSELF IN NONCOMPLEX AREAS, THEN YOU ARE HEADING TOWARDS COMPLEXITY. MEANING: IF YOU TRIED TO DEAL WITH EASY CRITERIA, YOU WILL FIND A WAY OUT FROM A SIMPLE PROBLEM BECAUSE YOU HARNESSED YOUR MIND TO DO EASY THINGS, <u>THEN WHEN YOU CONFRONT A COMPLEX PROBLEM, YOUR ONLY CHOICE WILL BY TRYING</u> TO ESCAPE SINCE YOUR MIND IS NOT ACCUSTOMED TO SOLVE THOSE HEAVY PROBLEMS. IT'S SIMILAR TO LEARNING TO SWIM IN A CALM SEA AND GAINED NO EXPERIENCE IN DEALING WITH ROUGH SEAS.

O Mind. Do you want to fly in a space full of bright stars? No worry, you can borrow wings. How are you going to borrow those wings? I know these are puzzling questions, yet the answer is: it's you who will borrow the wings from your own self, when you see the beauty of the word, when you look at the sky with the eyes of a bird. When you prove that you are capable to write a word that helps others. Make reading is your constant life style, it is only with your imagination that you can fly with the wings of your mind whenever you want. Read, Read and Read.

HOW TO BE A POSITIVE PERSON? WHEN YOU MEET NEGATIVE PERSONS AND KEEP ON THE SAME OPTIMISTIC WAY YOU ARE, NO MATTER HOW HARD THEY TRY TO DRAG YOU INTO THEIR SWAMP OF PESSIMISM LIKE HIGH WAVES THAT BREAKS WHILE YOU STAND LIKE A REEF ROCK, BECAUSE WHAT IS BUILT ON SOLID LAND CAN TOLERATE ANY SHAKE, WHILE WHAT IS BUILT ON SAND DUNES WILL NOT RESIST WINDS. BE POSITIVE AND DON'T KEEP YOURSELF IN THE TURMOIL OF MISERY.

WHEN YOU COVER YOUR EYES WITH YOUR HAND, YOU WILL ONLY VEIL THE SUN LIGHT FROM YOURSELF, WHILE THOSE AROUND YOU WILL SEE WHAT YOU DO. DON'T SKIP RULES AND REGULATIONS, AND DON'T HURT OTHERS FEELING, THOSE WHO ARE HURT, NEVER FORGET, WHILE THE ONE WHO HURTS USUALLY FORGETS, THIS IS A FACT, MANY PEOPLE DON'T CARE ABOUT OTHERS REACTIONS AS THEY DON'T REALIZE THE MAGNITUDE OF THEIR BAD ACTIVITIES WHEN ACTING WITH FOOLISHNESS. YOU WILL NOT FIND A PERSON WITH A BRAIN FULL OF AWARENESS AND CULTURE THAT BYPASSES SOCIETY BORDERS.

If there were schools that teach poems and love, then we wouldn't need to resort to the language of violence. Children acquire bad attitudes only when they enroll into schools of deprivation, hunger, poverty and loneliness.

Don't underestimate the straw in the mouth of a bird. The nest that shelters birds against <u>wind and rains</u> is made of straws. No one starts big. All began small and started to grow.

Setting among those with idle understanding men and women looks like a lion setting with cats. Despite they belong to the same species, but their shape and capabilities are different from that of a cat.

Don't lit candles under the sun light. It will add no more light. Oh, honest woman, don't talk to a dead person, he will never answer you. Those who don't know love will never know what is in your heart.

It is wise to be a giver, who wants nothing from the others, if the sea, would claim its rights, it wouldn't let fishermen leave with their fishing for nothing. Do the good and go without paying attention to the pockets of those you did well with them.

MONEY IS THE ENGINE THAT WILL
TAKE YOU TO YOUR WISHES. BUT,
DON'T FORGET THAT YOU ARE
STEERING THE WHEEL, IF YOU
HURRY WITH NO CONSIDERATION
FOR THE CONSEQUENCES, YOU MAY
CAUSE A SEVERE ACCIDENT. IF YOU
LOST YOUR MONEY, YOU WILL KNOW
YOUR FAITHFUL FRIENDS, WHO
WILL BE STAYING WITH YOU. SOME
LOSSES REVEAL THE REAL FACES.

WHEN A MAN IS LOOKING <u>AT</u> A
WOMAN AS A DELICIOUS BANQUET,
AND REMEMBERS HER ONLY WHEN
HE IS HUNGRY, THEN A <u>WOMAN</u>
<u>WILL LOOK AT MAN SAME WAY AS</u>
<u>THE OWNER OF A RESTAURANT</u>
LOOKS <u>AT</u> HIS CUSTOMERS
(WE LOVE OUR CUSTOMERS
BECAUSE THEY PAY MONEY)

Man's mind is in his tongue, the rose doesn't need to market for its scent, it is the breathe that spreads its scent, while the rose is standing still

The fish doesn't need to enroll in an institute to learn how to <u>swim</u>, its instinct does that <u>and</u> man has no choice in his shape, color or figure <u>when he</u> was born.

PATIENCE IS MAIN FEATURES OF
BEES TO <u>BUILD AND</u> COMPLETE A
HIVE AND FILL IT WITH HONEY,
HOW MANY FLOWERS ARE NEEDED
TO PRODUCE A HONEY THAT FILLS A
CUP? THIS CAN'T BE DONE WITHOUT
PATIENCE. MAN HAVE TO LEARN
THE BEES' PHILOSOPHY IN BUILDING
A BEEHIVE AND GET HONEY FROM
FLOWERS. DREAMS ARE NOT
FULFILLED IN A BLINK OF AN EYE.

Do you have money? Then you will be able to buy what you want to buy within the limits of what you got, and so, is the society. It will give <u>you</u> what you <u>deserve</u> based on how you deal with it. The <u>higher</u> your human balance, the more love you will get from the people to fulfill your demands.

Human balance is not to look for people's mistakes, especially those who suffer harsh conditions. We must not place them in the corner of sinners and judge them to satisfy our ego, <u>BECAUSE</u> tomorrow, we might be in their situation. Patience prior to making a decision is what we must consider.

WHEN YOU LOOK FROM ONE ANGLE
AND <u>IMPOSE</u> YOUR DECISION ON
THOSE AROUND YOU, THEN YOU ARE
SAILING WITH ONE RAW AND WILL
SAIL IN CIRCLES AND IT WILL BE
DIFFICULT TO REACH SAFE HARBORS.

IF A WOMAN WANTS TO SATISFY
HER MAN, SHE MUST QUIT FACE
MAKE UP AND FOCUS ON FOOD
MAKE UP. MOST MARRIED PEOPLE
PREFER THE BEAUTY OF FOOD THAN
THE BEAUTY OF THEIR WIVES.

Do you know that the ink of my pens can't write a single word without conscious or persistence?

MIND IS THE LEVEL OF SECRETIN

OF DEEP EXPERIENCES.

MONEY <u>DIRTS</u> CAN'T
STAIN CLEAN LOVE.

TOLERANCE IS THE BASIS OF
BUILDING A LIFE BASED ON
GOOD PARENTAL VALUES.

Every long lasting deed is the product of a conscious living on credibility.

The wings of lights are showered from skies of light that folds the horizons of holiness that we don't realize to spread the warm rays of sun over the bright clouds.

Golden Letters

In the sense that my philosophical tendencies will carry
every spiritual and pictorial dimension that focuses on the
movement of things after giving them the impetus of life

In the eyes of the poet, everything is a living
creature, but it has an underlying system

I see those subtleties with the eyes of my
mind and not with my naked eyes.
I mean that my next stories and novels will be this
way and better after someone translates them
who can handle creative translation tools.

When the old night reclined to rest from the
practice of repeating the blackness, in preparation
for the arrival of the birth of a new dawn,

The old man's steps were like a tortoise heading up.

The old man stood looking at the blind lamp. Then he
nodded, saying: I see you, lamp, have lost your sight

and such a night has receded, which is about to withdraw
from this worldly plate..you are like the lips of a stupid gun
that never a pronounce a single shot in the ear of battle.

A bird cuts the thread of meditation for the old man

After he climbed the pine tree that shaded the
house's eye, which is its only window.

A lukewarm smile slowly appears on the old man's lips,
as dawn advances with the steps of a return from an
old travel, the bird joins, leaving the pine branch, with
swarms of migrating birds, leaving the tree repeating
the tales of shadows for the old man when the sun
sees and sees existence with an eye of pure light.

When words wake up from the bed of ignorance, the awakening of certainty takes them to minds wishing to reflect and learn, and with that bold awakening dissipated Fragments of the illusions of the night of naivety that lengthened its darkness over the heads of the lost in the slumber of false dreams. Therefore, those who want to get out of the prisons of unconsciousness should turn to the free deep word, It is the immortal pen that forges the gold of letters

TO ADORN THE NECKS OF MINDS
WITH JEWELS OF NOBLE MEANINGS.

THE TALK OF PURE REASON DOES NOT
STOP AT POINTING THE FINGER OF
CRITICISM AND CONSCIOUS WISDOM
IN A SARCASTIC OR SOMETIMES
HUMOROUS WAY, WITH THE AIM OF
MATURING THE GROWTH OF CARE,
IN ORDER TO SATISFY THE HUNGER
OF THE MIND THAT FEEDS ON THE
FRUITS OF ADVICE, AS THESE ARE THE
PILLARS OF HUMAN SURVIVAL IN THE
FORM OF RATIONAL LOGIC, IN ORDER
TO MANAGE PROBLEMS IN THE MOST
APPROPRIATE AND OPTIMAL MANNER.

SOME HEARTS ARE LIKE A HEATER

WHICH BURNS TO GIVE
WARMTH TO OTHERS

IN THE END, IT WILL BE
DESTINED FOR ASHES

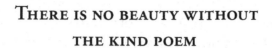

THERE IS NO BEAUTY WITHOUT
THE KIND POEM

THIS IS A FACT THAT IDIOTS DO NOT ACCEPT

HAVE YOU FORGOTTEN, O WORLD, THAT
THE SEA DOES NOT RECEIVE MONEY
WHEN ITS SAVINGS ARE STOLEN?

WHEN WILL YOU BE AS GENEROUS AS THE WIDE SEA!?

EVERY UNFORTUNATE PERSON COMES
TO POWER BY THE DEVIL

THERE IS ONLY ONE WAY TO RETURN
TO PURE CONSCIENCE

IT CONSISTS IN ABANDONING EVIL AND
APPREHENDING WITH THE HAND OF SALVATION

DON'T BE SAD, MY DISTANT FRIEND

THERE ARE GOOD THINGS LOOMING ON THE
HORIZON COMING FROM THE SKY OF GOOD

AND WHEN WORDS ESCAPE FROM THE
ETERNAL PRISONS OF BOOKS

THE FLOWER WILL COME FROM THE BOAT OF THE
CLOUDS TO FLOAT OVER THE LAND FREE OF
BLOOD, HATRED AND BLACK HYPOCRISY).

SAVE ME, HOLY LIGHT!
THE DARKNESS OF SADNESS SURROUNDS MY
TIRED SOUL FROM THE LONG MYSTERY
I STAND ON THE MUD OF LOSS
THE WORLD SWAYED ME
I ONLY FIND STABILITY IN THE SUBCONSCIOUS MIND
HOW CAN THINGS LEAVE THINGS?
AND HOW DO LOVERS ABANDON THEIR MEMORIES
FOR THE SAKE OF FRIGHTENING FALSEHOOD?
WORDS STILL WANDER IN THE DESERT OF IGNORANCE THIRSTY
IN A WORLD FULL OF MODERNITY AND MACHINERY
AWAY FROM THE TOUCHES OF WARMTH AND THE
REASSURING GLANCES OF TENDERNESS
DID THE STEPS OF LONGING LEAVE THE PATH
OF LOVERS WITHOUT RETURN?
DID THE SEAGULL ABANDON THE DREAMS OF HARBORS
AND LEAVE THE SHORES LISTENING TO THE MOURNFUL
ROAR OF THE WAVES, IN THE ABSENCE OF ALL THE WINGS
THAT SANG YESTERDAY THE SONG OF ETERNAL PEACE?
AND YOU, MY DISTANT FRIEND MILLER,
HOW DID MY MUTE WORDS FIND THEIR
WAY INTO YOUR CONSCIOUS EARS?
HOW CAN LETTERS ESCAPE FROM THE PRISON OF
PAPER TO THE PATH OF ABSOLUTE FREEDOM?!
I KNOW THAT THE NIGHT DOES NOT SEE THE LAMPS
AND I KNOW THAT DUST DOES NOT SPEAK EXCEPT
IN THE FACE OF THE WIND THAT PROVOKES
IT'S A STRANGE WORLD
FOR THE SAKE OF MONEY WE BUILT A TEMPLE, AND OUR
FOREHEADS PROSTRATED IN HOPE OF THE SHRINE OF THE CREED
AND FOR BLIND FUN
WE HAVE SEEN THE PATH OF MINDLESS MISTAKES
EVERYTHING MOVES UP TO THE STONE
BUT ONLY THE POETS WHO ARE SUSPENDED BETWEEN CERTAINTY
AND DOUBT UNDERSTAND THIS MYSTERIOUS HADITH.

Paths without steps

GIVE ME, O BRIDE OF HEAVEN, YOUR SILKY WINGS

THE SMOKE OF LIFE DOES NOT CALM DOWN FROM THE
BLOWING OF GRUDGES AGAINST THE WORLDS

IS THERE A HOLE TO ESCAPE FROM THE VASTNESS
OF FEAR TO THE NARROWNESS OF SAFETY?

OUR DREAMS STILL STAND AFRAID BEHIND
THE WINDOWS OF THE DISTANT NIGHT

SILENTLY WATCHING US TIRED

THERE IS A PURE FACE THAT PRAYS FOR
THE SALVATION OF ALL PEOPLE

AND THERE ARE THE FANGS OF DEMONS

THAT WATCHES THE UNWARY

FOR A MOMENT OF EVIL ONSLAUGHT

THIS IS THE PHILOSOPHY OF LIFE HIDDEN IN THE BOOK
THE SEEING HEART AND THE BLIND KNIFE

DO WE UNDERSTAND HOW THE SEASONS OF OUR FLUCTUATING
MOODS PROCEED WITHOUT KNOWING THE IRRITANTS?

ARE WE AWARE THAT LIFE HAS A GLORY THAT
ONLY THE TOLERANT CAN ATTAIN?

CAN WE BE WITH THE BENEFACTORS?

WE WILL BE GREAT WITH THE PURITY OF OUR HEARTS WHEN
WE KNOW THAT LIFE IS SHORTER THAN SUNSET, SO WHY

WE ARE AT WAR WITH EACH OTHER FOR WHATEVER REASON.

ONE DAY OUR BRILLIANCE MAY FADE

THE BURDENS OF CIRCUMSTANCES
MAY PILE UP ON OUR SHOULDERS

WE ONLY FIND OUR MINDS
WITH US TO RELIEVE US OF
ALL OUR LONG WORRIES.

Spinning in the immortal poem

I SEE THE MOON SHINING UNTIL IT STEALS FROM
THE BRIGHTNESS OF YOUR CHEEK A PURE LIGHT
AND SHE BORROWS THE SUN TO COLOR HER
LUMINOUS STRANDS THE COLOR OF BLOND
GOLD FROM YOUR PERFUMED HAIR
AND ALL THE BUTTERFLIES FLY AROUND
YOU TO TELL YOU THAT YOU ARE THE MOST
BEAUTIFUL UNDER THE SKY OF THE WORLD
AND WHEN YOU WALK, O LIKENESS OF ANGELS,
ALL THE CURVATURES OF THE ROADS TURN INTO A
STRAIGHT PATH BEFORE YOUR CONFIDENT STEPS
AND THE PATH BECOMES STRAIGHT, SHY AND HUMBLE,
SO AS NOT TO CAUSE YOU TROUBLE, BABE
AND ALL THE EMOTIONAL WORDS ESCAPE
FROM THE BOOKS OF POETS
AND TURNS INTO AN EMERALD NECKLACE
TO ENCIRCLE YOUR NECK WITH A WREATH OF JASMINE.
STONES HURT WHEN YOU STEP ON THEM,
ETERNAL QUEEN OF HEAVEN
NOT BECAUSE YOU STEPPED ON IT, BUT BECAUSE THE
STONE WAS AFRAID TO HURT YOUR SOFT FEET
AND WHEN YOU TOUCH THE WIDE SEA
SALT WATER GETS DIABETES
BECAUSE YOU ARE THE SWEETEST HONEY
THE BEES LEAVE THE HILLS AND HEAD TOWARDS
THE SEA THAT YOU HAVE TOUCHED, THE MOST
BEAUTIFUL WOMEN IN THE WORLD.
EVEN INSANE TORNADOES FALL QUIETLY
BEFORE YOUR INFINITE BEAUTY
AND SWAYING LIKE A SPRING BREEZE BEHIND
YOUR BRAIDS LIKE A CHILD.

MORE WOMEN WILL GO TO
THE MONEY TEMPLE
TO PRAY TO THE GODDESS OF LUXURY
AND THEY WILL WEEP IN
SUPPLICATION UNTIL THE GODS OF
MONEY RESPOND TO THEM AND THE
HEAVENS SEND MONEY OVER THEM.

WHEN THE EYES OF LOVE ARE CLOSED
THE WORLD TURNS BLIND

WHEN WOMEN WITH BEAUTIFUL
BODIES GO OUT TO THE BEACHES
THE SEAGULLS WILL SEND A CHIRP
TO THE TRAITOROUS MEN

ON THE PRETEXT THAT THE OFFICIAL
HOLIDAY WEEKEND NEEDS AN EXCUSE
TO FEED THE SEAGULLS (HUMANE
WORK - ANIMAL WELFARE)

If pride enters the life of the spouses
Love will come out servile and broken
Some hasty decisions need train brakes

Dilated pupils do not mean that a
person monitors and knows everything
that is going on around him
Many people with big eyes
only see their shoes
Not everything that appears
reflects the truth

Of course there are some romantic
relationships that are
Like visiting rain: rare
Also, on the contrary, there
are relationships like a
continuous flowing river
Of course you went through the above
Tell the truth please.

It is shameful to make our

ears like a landfill

Filled with all mold and filth

Is it our job to gossip?

So what did we leave for

the newscast then?

It is good for us to

deliver the good news

Instead of causing

hearts to separate and

scattering their dreams

Tell her he loves her

And tell her that she loves you

Even if it wasn't true

MANY BOOKS SUFFER
FROM PAPER OBESITY
BUT ITS CONTENT SUFFERS FROM
A DEFICIENCY IN THE VITAMIN
OF KNOWLEDGE AND NEEDS THE
REINFORCEMENTS OF SOBER SCIENCE
NOT EVERY GREAT BOOK REFLECTS
THE GREATNESS OF KNOWLEDGE
JUST A REMINDER.

WHEN DO WE LEARN
TRANSCENDENCE FROM THE PALM
TREES FACING THE HORIZON?
AND WHEN DO WE LEARN FROM
SILK TO SUBORDINATE OUR
FEELINGS TO THOSE WE LOVE?
AND WHEN WILL WE LEARN TO
HIDE OUR SECRETS LIKE A MISER
WHO HIDES HIS MONEY FROM
THE EYES OF THE WORLDS.

IF YOU SHOUT AT A STONE, IT
WILL NEVER MOVE IN RESPONSE
TO YOUR COMMAND
SO DO PEOPLE WHO SPEND
THEIR LIVES IN DISCOTHEQUES
AND PRISONS
SHUT UP PLEASE

ALL THE VARIOUS TREES
ARE CLOSE TO EACH OTHER
IN THE FOREST WITHOUT
BOREDOM OR COMPETITION
(ENVIRONMENTAL COEXISTENCE)
THERE ARE THORNY TREES
THERE ARE ALSO PEACEFUL TREES
THORNY TREES DO NOT LEAVE THEIR
ROOTS UNTIL THEY HARM THE
TALLEST TREES OR THOSE AROUND
THEM ON THE PRETEXT THAT THEY
ARE CHARACTERIZED BY FRUIT
WHEN WILL WE HUMANS
LEARN THE PHILOSOPHY OF
FOREST TREES IN THE WAYS OF
COEXISTENCE AND CLOSENESS?

IF EVERY HUNDRED PEOPLE SET

UP A FUND FOR THE PURPOSE

OF HELPING THE POOR

THERE WILL BE NO POOR

IN THIS WORLD

IS THAT CHOICE TOO DIFFICULT?

SO, LET US WORK UNTIL WE LIE IN

OUR BED WITH A CONSCIENCE FULL

OF COMFORT AND CONTENTMENT

BECAUSE WE CREATE

HAPPINESS FOR THE NEEDY.

THERE ARE WOMEN WHO KEEP A
MEMORY LIKE THAT OF ELEPHANTS
AND THERE ARE MEN WHOSE
MEMORY IS LIKE THAT OF FISH
WOMEN DO NOT FORGET THE
BETRAYAL OF MEN
WHILE MEN FORGET THEIR
BETRAYAL OF THEIR WOMEN.

THE CLOSER WE GET TO THE FIRE,
THE MORE HEAT WE FEEL
AND AS WE MOVE AWAY FROM THE
STOVE, WE EMBRACE WINTER
A PERSON SHOULD BE CLOSE
TO HIS BROTHERHOOD
TO COMPLETE THE PICTURE OF
FRATERNITY AND COOPERATION
A TREE FAR FROM THE SOURCE
OF WATER DOES NOT GROW
WE MEET WITH LOVE.

SOME MEN ARE STILL AFRAID
OF HOSPITAL NEEDLES
BUT THEY ARE NOT AFRAID OF
STEALING OTHER PEOPLE'S IDEAS
(CONTRADICTORY WORLD)
-A HAT DOES NOT PREVENT
THOUGHTS FROM ESCAPING FROM
THE HEADS OF THE IGNORANT
BUT IT PREVENTS THE ARRIVAL
OF VITAMIN D FROM FEEDING THE
HEADS OF THE IGNORANT ONLY.

WHEN WE EAT WITH A SILVER

SPOON OR A WOODEN SPOON

WE WILL FEEL FULL

THEY BOTH SERVE THE

SAME PURPOSE

WHY DO WE LIE TO OURSELVES?

IN A WORLD FULL OF

HUNGRY PEOPLE?

The safe is made to hide valuables
As the earth hides all its
valuable savings in its interior
Why should we expose all
our possessions to others in
order to entice thieves and
motivate the envious and the
disadvantaged against us?
And then we cry because
we were robbed
Let us be like the treasury
and like the earth.

A DOCTOR ASKED A HEALTHY PERSON:
HAVE YOU MET THE CORONA VIRUS?
THE YOUNG MAN REPLIED: NO,
DOCTOR, WE HAVEN'T MET YET
THE DOCTOR REPLIED: THAT'S
FORTUNATE FOR YOU
THE YOUNG DOCTOR ASKED AGAIN: IS
THERE ANYONE IN YOUR HOUSE ABOUT
WHOM YOU FEAR THE PANDEMIC?
THE YOUNG MAN REPLIED: HE
IS MY GRANDFATHER
THE DOCTOR SAID IN A FAINT VOICE:
ARE YOU NOT AFRAID THAT YOU WILL BE
THE REASON FOR THE ABSENCE OF YOUR
GRANDFATHER FROM THE BOARD OF LIFE
BY TRANSMITTING THE VIRUS TO HIM?
THE YOUNG MAN LOWERED HIS HEAD,
THEN RAISED IT, AND WITH A CONVICTION
ON HIS FACE, HE SAID TO THE DOCTOR:
WHERE IS THE VACCINATION ROOM?
THE YOUNG MAN TURNED AFTER
LIFTING HIS SHIRT OFF HIS FOREARM,
PREPARING TO TAKE THE VACCINE
LET'S ALL GO TOWARDS RECOVERY THEN.

Towards the future All of our
goals are looking forward to
reaching the highest ranks
There are those who strive
and work hard and persevere
without stopping
And there are climbers who ride
the waves of success effortlessly
So that they are with us
in the first ranks.
Therefore, the wise should
strip the intrusive dependants
and put them in the light
instead of hiding in the dark to
steal the efforts of others.
They should be charged with the
professional and cultural cost
Until they are put in a societal
test, they either pass or fail.

WHEN YOUR ANGELIC FACE HIDES

FROM THE MIRROR OF MY EYES

ALL OUR IMAGES ESCAPE FROM THE

FRAME OF MEMORY TO THE SKIES

OF DIASPORA AND FADING

BETWEEN MY DREAMS AND YOUR

DREAMS ARE TIRED FANTASIES

HOW DID YOU MAKE THE RAIN

FALL AT YOUR FEET?

HOW DID YOU CAPTURE THE HEARTS OF

LOVERS WITHOUT WAR OR RESTRICTIONS?

THE ROTATION OF LONGING DOES NOT STOP

AND THE MADNESS OF LOVE DOES NOT REST

AND THE CRY OF THE LONELY DOES

NOT STOP UNTIL AFTER HE TOUCHES

YOUR HANDS, MY DISTANT BRIDE

ON THE ALTAR OF LOVE, I LIT PRAYER CANDLES

AND ON THE TILES OF THE TEMPLES

I SHED TEARS OF FORGIVENESS

IF FATE

MY HEART, SINCE TOUCHING YOUR KINDNESS,

HAS BEEN IMPRISONED BEHIND YOUR

RIB CAGE, IMPRISONED FOR LIFE

THE BIRDS OF LONGING COME
TO STAND ON THE SWAYING
BRANCHES OF WAITING
WHEN THE SKY OPENS ITS DOORS,
THE LIGHT COMES DOWN IN
THE FORM OF A SHADOW
SPRING FILLS ME WITH THE
COLORS OF THE GRASS
AND MY EYES TURN INTO A BREEDING
GROUND FOR COLORFUL BUTTERFLIES
THE FRAGRANT JASMINE FLOWER
GROWS AT THE TIPS OF MY FINGERS
AND NOSTALGIA GROWS IN THE
CRADLE OF NOBLE EMOTIONS
AND THE DREAMY SEASONS
OF LOVE ARE RENEWED
AND THE NIGHT RETURNS, SITS
WITH THE CANDLES OF LISTENS
TO THE TALES OF THE LOVERS.

AS IN THE MICROSCOPIC ENVIRONMENT THAT
CANNOT BE SEEN WITH THE NAKED EYE

THERE ARE ALSO DISGUISED HUMANS WHO PLAY THE ROLE OF MICROBES

THEY STEAL AND SABOTAGE BECAUSE WE ARE UNABLE TO MONITOR
THEM AND BECAUSE THEY HIDE IN TECHNOLOGICAL INVISIBILITY

WHAT IS THE SOLUTION THEN TO GET RID
OF HARMFUL HUMAN MICROBES?

AS IN THE MICROSCOPIC ENVIRONMENT THAT
CANNOT BE SEEN WITH THE NAKED EYE

THERE ARE ALSO DISGUISED HUMANS WHO PLAY THE ROLE OF MICROBES

THEY STEAL AND SABOTAGE BECAUSE WE ARE UNABLE TO MONITOR
THEM AND BECAUSE THEY HIDE IN TECHNOLOGICAL INVISIBILITY

WHAT IS THE SOLUTION THEN TO GET RID
OF HARMFUL HUMAN MICROBES?

HUMAN RELATIONS MUST BE STERILIZED WITH
DISINFECTANTS OF CAUTION AND CAUTION

AND THAT WE ALWAYS RENEW OUR CONFIDENCE IN
OURSELVES MORE THAN WE TRUST IN STRANGERS

ADHERENCE TO THE CAUTIONARY GUIDELINES REGARDING
INTELLECTUAL PROPERTY DOCUMENTATION

IT SHOULD BE IN PAPER FORM, NOT ELECTRONICALLY.

HUMAN RELATIONS MUST BE STERILIZED WITH DISINFECTANTS

ANTISEPTICS COMPOSED OF THE COMPONENT OF ATTENTION.

AND AN ELEMENT OF CAUTION.

AND THAT WE ALWAYS RENEW OUR CONFIDENCE IN
OURSELVES MORE THAN WE TRUST IN STRANGERS

ADHERENCE TO THE CAUTIONARY GUIDELINES REGARDING
INTELLECTUAL PROPERTY DOCUMENTATION

IT SHOULD BE IN PAPER FORM, NOT ELECTRONICALLY.

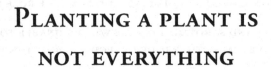

PLANTING A PLANT IS
NOT EVERYTHING

YOU HAVE TO WATER YOUR
PLANT UNTIL IT GROWS

AND THAT'S NOT ALL

YOU MUST FENCE YOUR PLANT
SO THAT IT IS NOT TOUCHED
BY THIEVES AND VANDALS

WHEN YOUR PLANT GROWS
AND BECOMES A TREE

YOUR TURN WILL BE OVER

SO ARE OUR CHILDREN WITH THE
SAME PHILOSOPHY AS THE PLANT

REVIVING THE AFFLICTED REQUIRES
AN OPTIMISM-TYPE CRANE WHOSE
ENGINES RUN ON THE FUEL OF HOPE
UNTIL THE PSYCHOLOGICALLY
BROKEN PEOPLE ARE BROUGHT
OUT FROM THE BOTTOM OF
DESPAIR TO THE VASTNESS
OF THE HAPPY WORLD.

A COUPLE'S LOVE BEGINS LIKE A MODERN FIRE

AND AFTER THE PASSAGE OF TIME ON THE WOOD, WHICH
IS THE FEELINGS ON WHICH THE FIRE FEEDS, THE HEAT
AND STRENGTH OF THE FLAME AND WARMTH SUBSIDE

AND AFTER MORE AND MORE TIME PASSED,
THE FIRE COOLED AND THE STOVE WAS
COVERED WITH A COVER OF ASH

AND IT ENDS

THIS IS SIMILAR TO MOST MARITAL RELATIONSHIPS

SO THE HEAT OF LOVE AND FEELINGS ARE
STRONG BEFORE MEETING THE BODIES

IF WE IMAGINE THAT THE BODIES
TAKE THE PLACE OF WOOD

AND AFTER THEY MARRY, THE GLOW OF LOVE COOLS

AND THE STATE OF ASHES BEGINS TO INVADE
THE HEARTH OF MARRIED LIFE

UNTIL THE SUPREME RELATIONSHIP BECOMES ASHES

AND THE REST OF THE ROLE IS ON THE WIND

ANY PROBLEMS

CRISES BLOW FROM THE MOUTHS OF BOREDOM,
BETRAYAL AND BOREDOM IN THE TRUMPET OF
SEPARATION, AND FAMILIES ARE SCATTERED
LIKE ASHES WITHOUT RETURNING.

Printed in the United States
by Baker & Taylor Publisher Services